# PENCIL, PAPER, DRAW!®
# DOGS

# STEVE HARPSTER

STERLING CHILDREN'S BOOKS
New York

This book is dedicated to my supportive and loving wife, Karen, who was nice enough
to practice drawing the dogs on these pages.

STERLING CHILDREN'S BOOKS
New York

An Imprint of Sterling Publishing
387 Park Avenue South
New York, NY 10016

Text and illustrations © 2006 by Steve Harpster

Previously published in a different format by Sterling Publishing Co., Inc. in 2006.

ISBN 978-1-4549-1152-4

Distributed in Canada by Sterling Publishing
C/o Canadian Manda Group, 165 Dufferin Street
Toronto, Ontario, Canada M6K 3H6
Distributed in the United Kingdom by GMC Distribution Services
Castle Place, 166 High Street, Lewes, East Sussex, England BN7 1XU
Distributed in Australia by Capricorn Link (Australia) Pty. Ltd.
P.O. Box 704, Windsor, NSW 2756, Australia

For information about custom editions, special sales, and premium and corporate purchases,
please contact Sterling Special Sales at 800-805-5489 or specialsales@sterlingpublishing.com.

Manufactured in China
Lot #:
2  4  6  8  10  9  7  5  3  1
02/14

www.sterlingpublishing.com/kids

# Contents

# Introduction

Drawing is a lot of fun and a great hobby. You can draw alone or with friends. Draw while watching television or quietly in the library at school. Take a pad of paper and some pencils on a long car trip to pass the time. Keep in mind that drawing is just like playing music, sports, or learning state capitals, it takes practice. Don't expect to be great on the first try. You will learn more and more each time you draw. By putting the date on the bottom or back of your drawings, you can keep track of your progress. Hang your drawings up in your room so you can look at them and see what you can improve on. Just have fun drawing and you will see your drawing skills improve each day.

# How to Use This Book

You will notice there are different colored lines in each drawing step. Blue lines are the new steps. Black lines are the lines done in a previous step and gray lines are lines not needed in the final drawing.

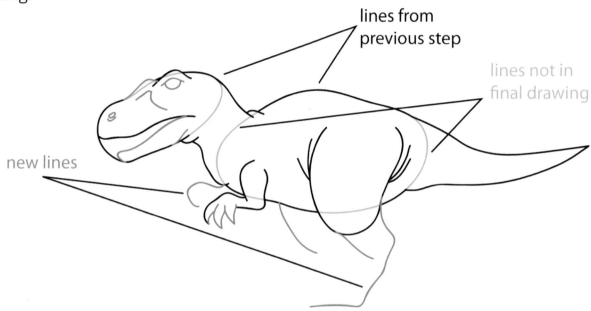

lines from
previous step

lines not in
final drawing

new lines

When you first start drawing make sure to draw very light. Many of the shapes and lines you start with are guides and will not be needed in the finished drawing.

You don't need to erase the gray lines in each step as you draw.  In the final step press harder with your pencil and trace over the lines want to keep. You can even go over the final step with a black pen.

A trick that most artists use when drawing is a sheet of tracing paper. Sketch your drawing following the steps in the book. When you are finished lay a sheet of tracing paper over your finished sketch. Now trace over the lines you want to keep in your final drawing.

 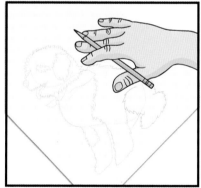 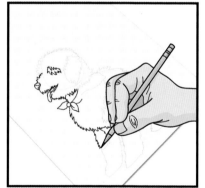 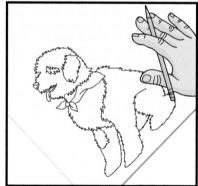

After following the steps in this book try drawing something that's not in this book. You should learn to view animals, people, or machines as a group of many shapes and lines. When you begin to see how simple shapes and lines combine to create form you will be well on your way to drawing anything you want. Hope you have fun learning to draw and remember, practice makes perfect.

# Draw a Basset Hound

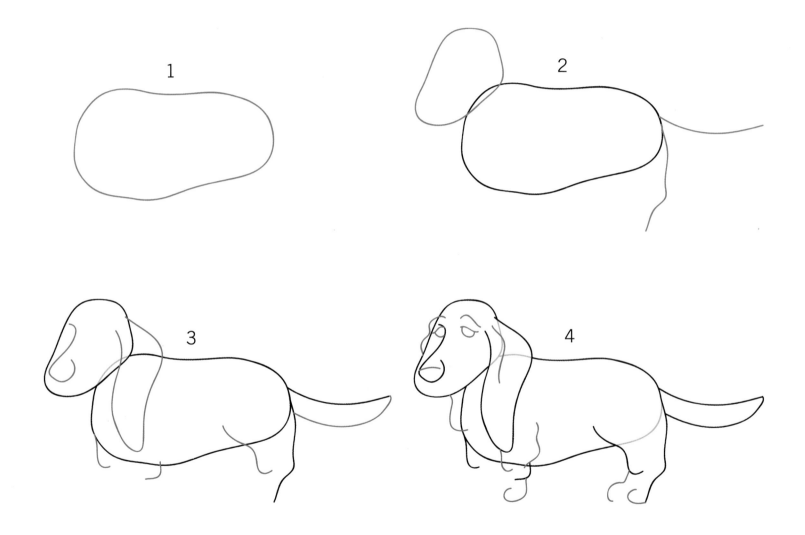

1

2

3

4

5

6

7

8

# Draw a German Shepherd

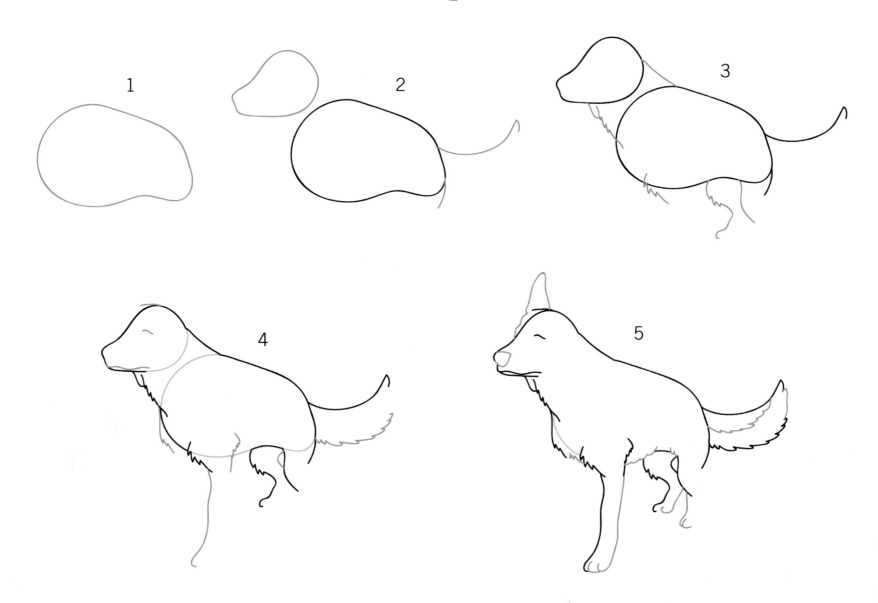

1

2

3

4

5

10

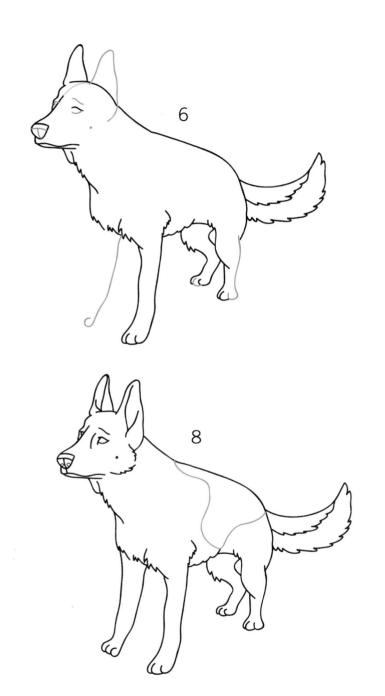

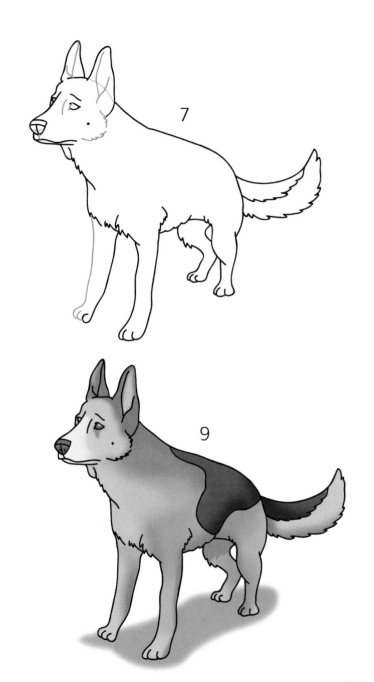

**11**

# Draw a Bull Terrier

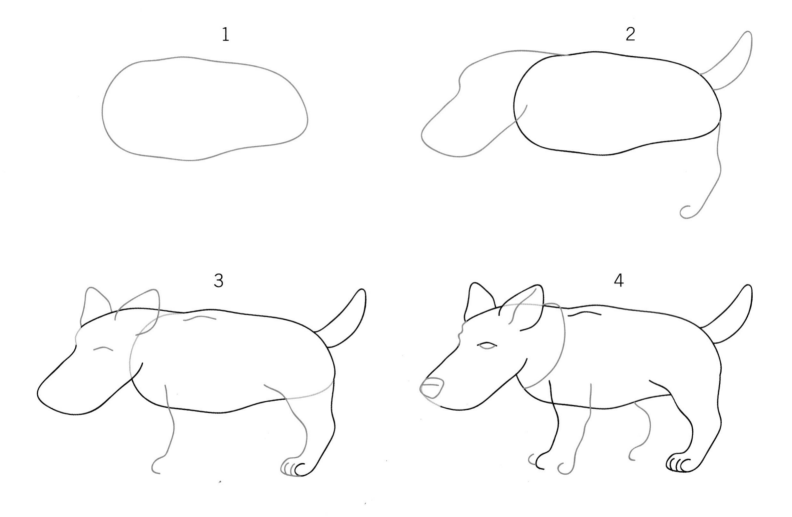

1

2

3

4

# Draw a Cairn Terrier

1

2

3

4

5

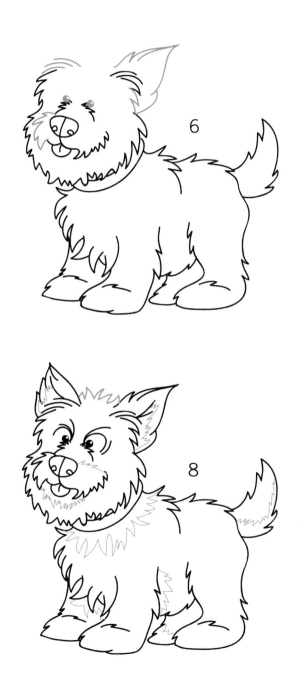

6

7

8

9

15

# Draw a Cocker Spaniel

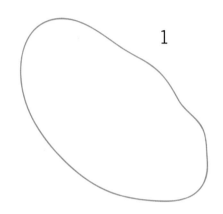

1

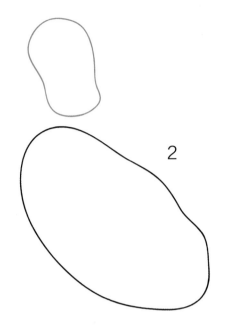

2

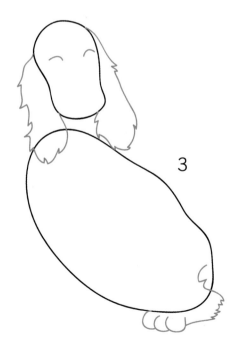

3

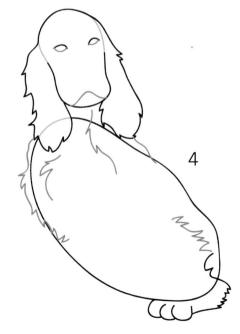

4

16

5

6

7

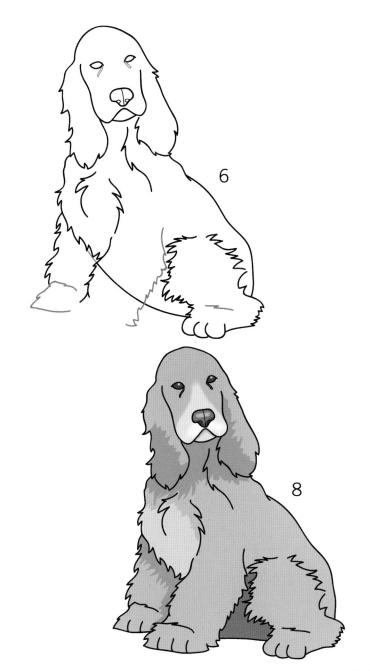

8

# Draw a Dalmation

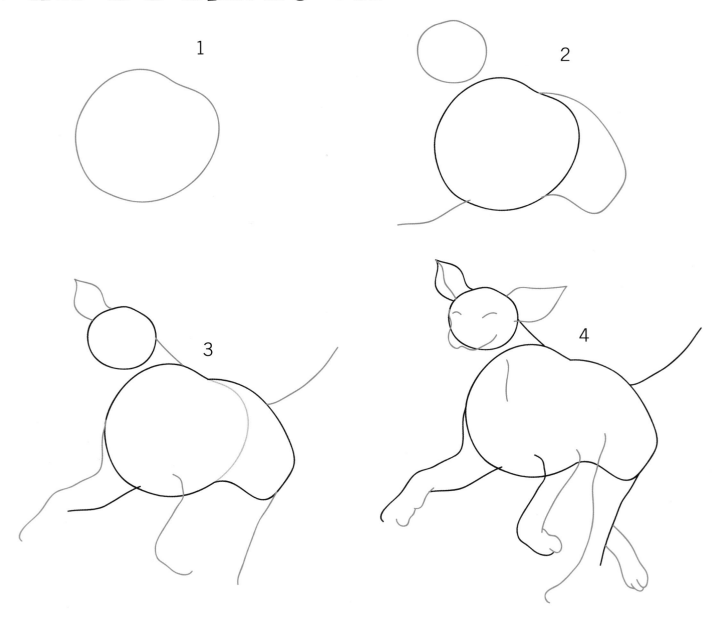

1

2

3

4

# Draw a Doberman

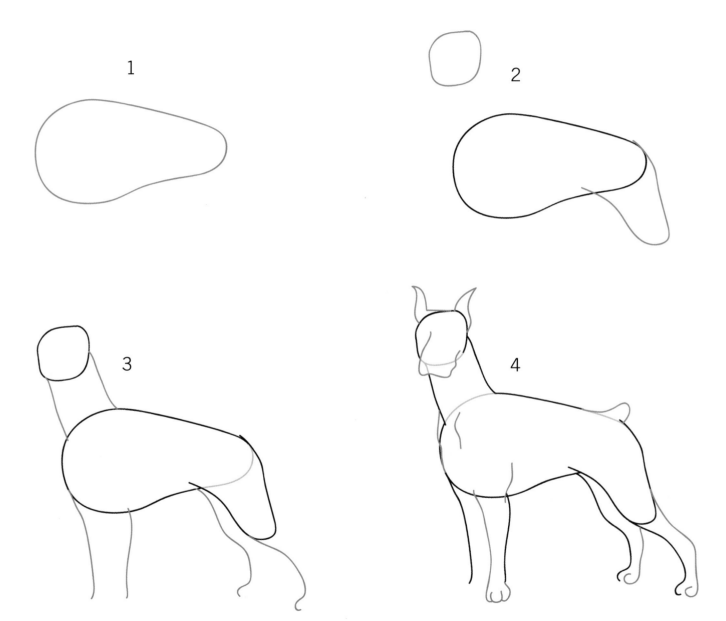

1

2

3

4

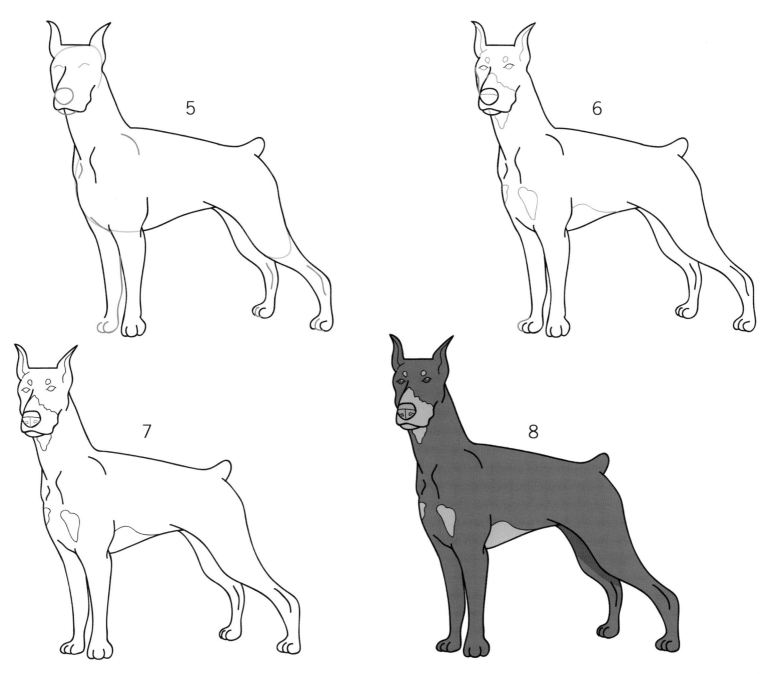

5

6

7

8

# Draw an Eskimo Dog

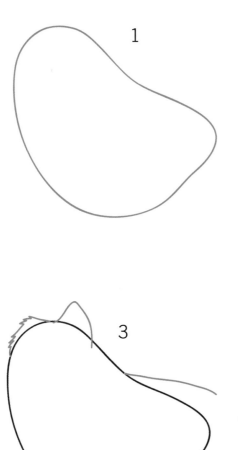

1

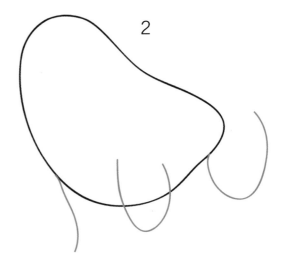

2

3

4

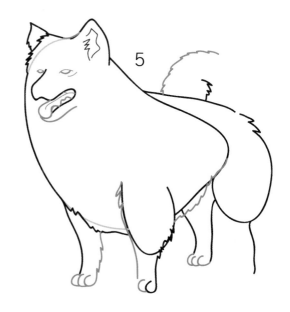

5

6

7

8

# Draw a Fox Terrier

1

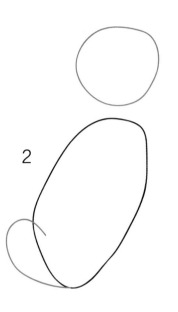

2

3

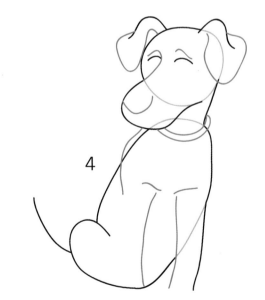

4

5

6

7

8

# Draw a Foxhound

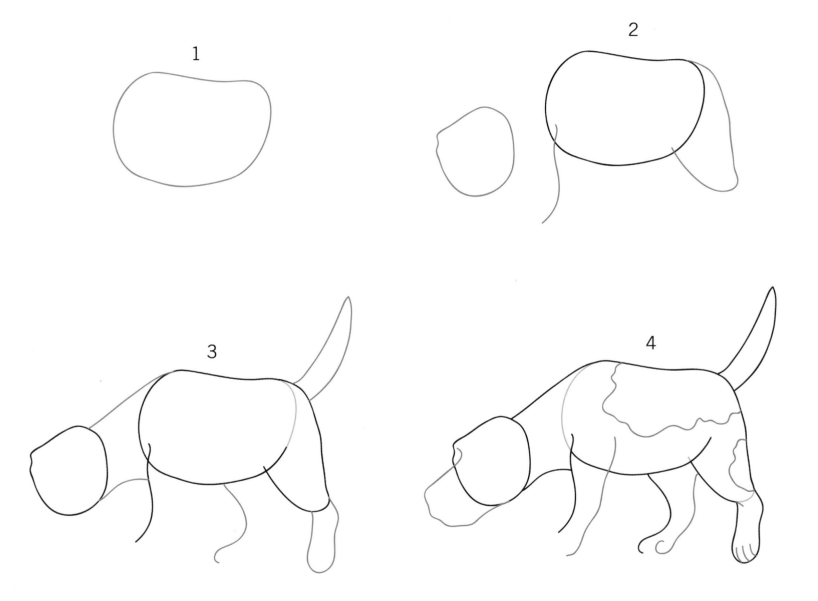

1

2

3

4

5

6

7

8

**27**

# Draw a Great Dane

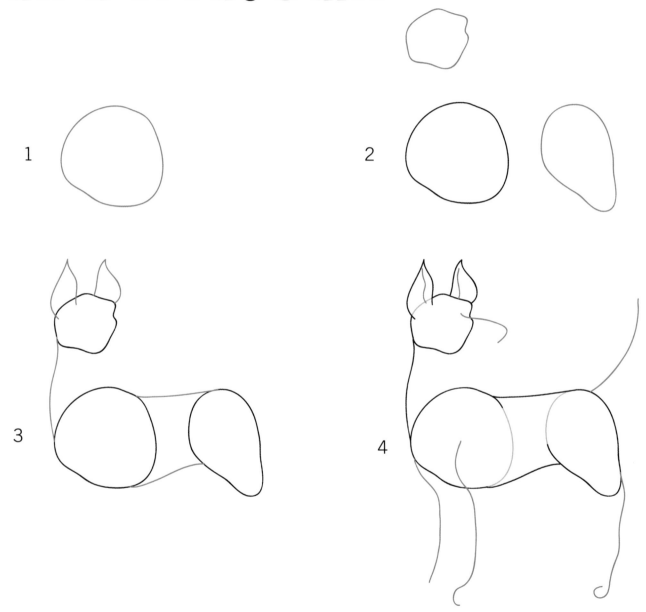

5

6

7

# Draw a Greyhound

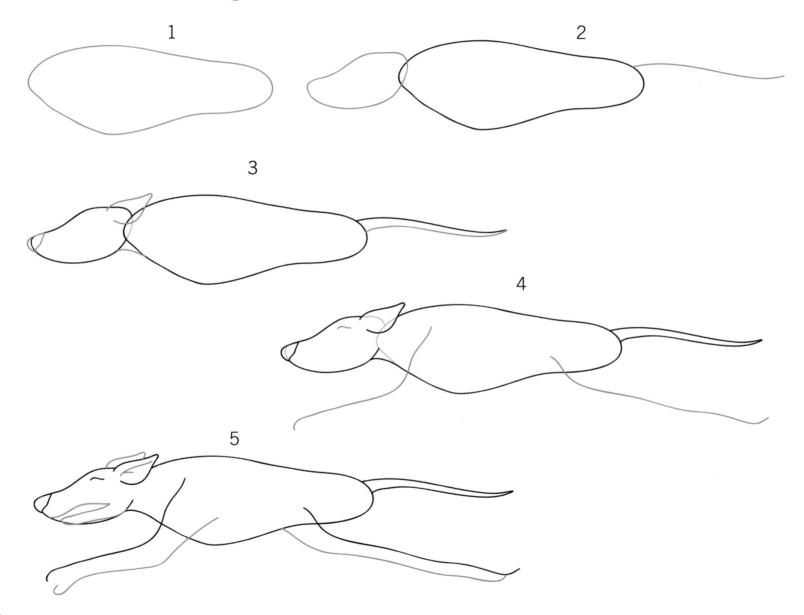

1

2

3

4

5

6

7

8

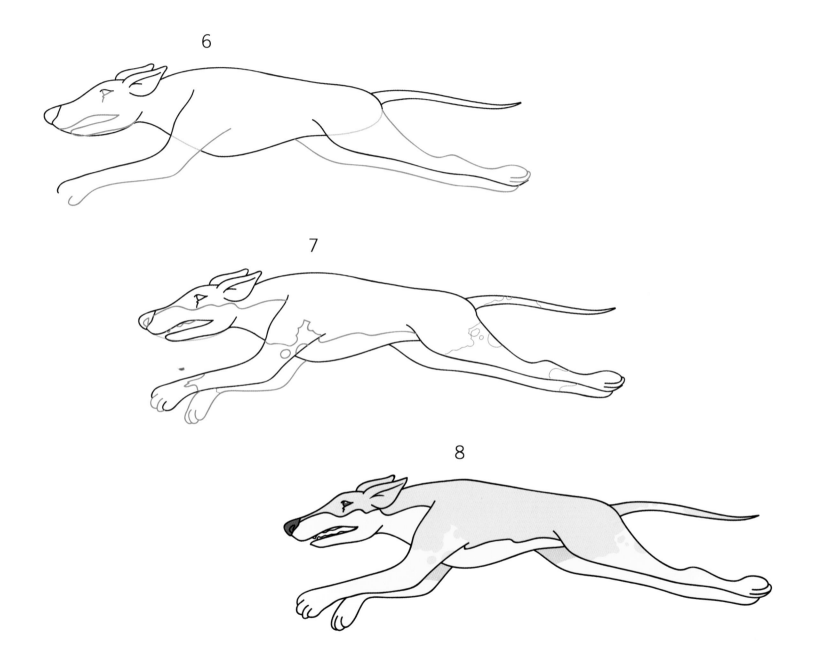

# Draw an Irish Setter

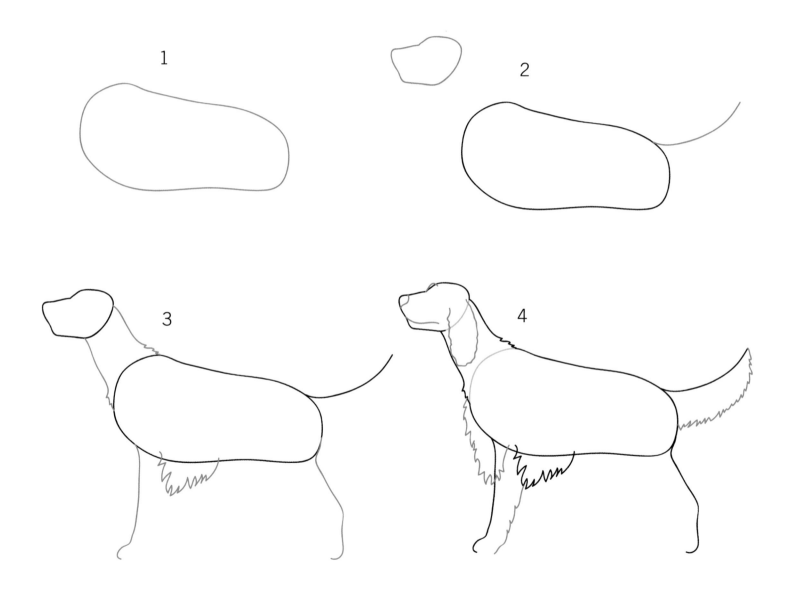

5

6

7

**33**

# Draw a Labrador Retriever

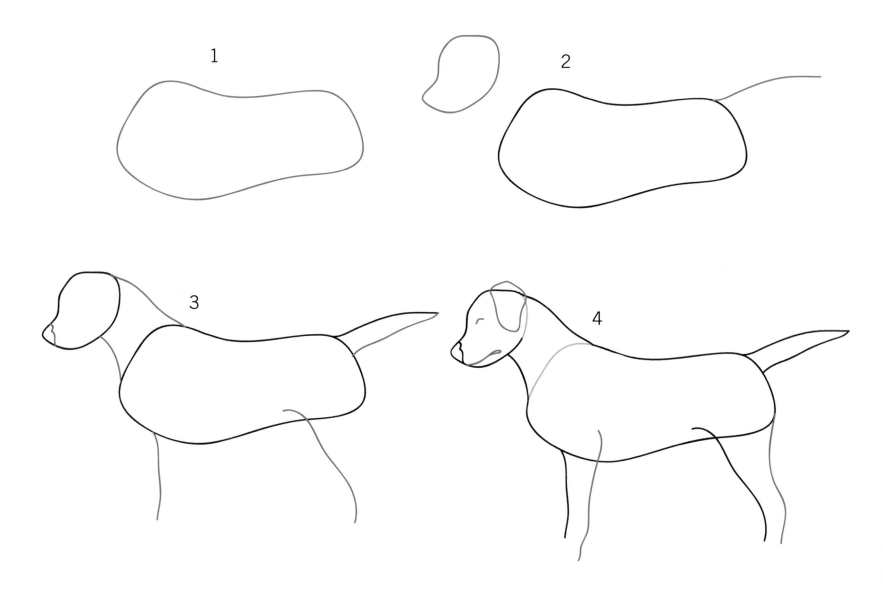

1

2

3

4

5

6

7

# Draw a Newfoundland

1

2

3

4

5

6

7

8

# Draw a Poodle

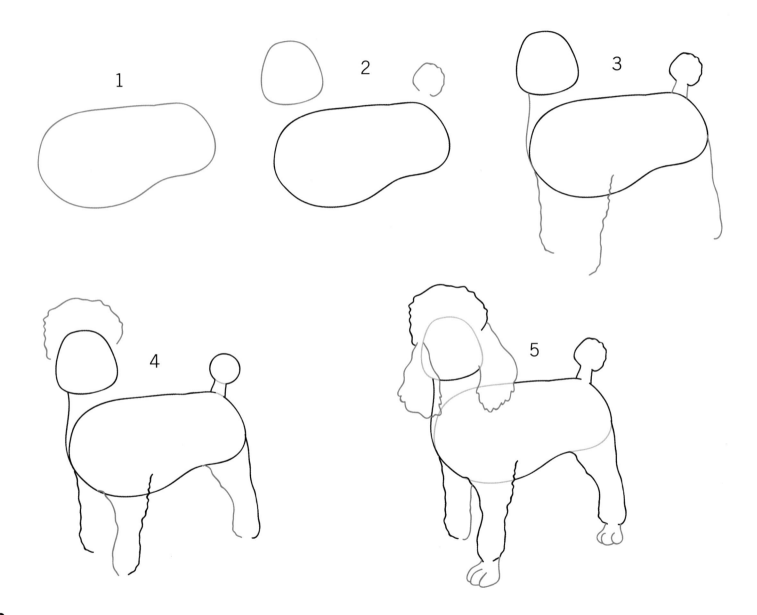

1
2
3
4
5

# Draw a Saint Bernard

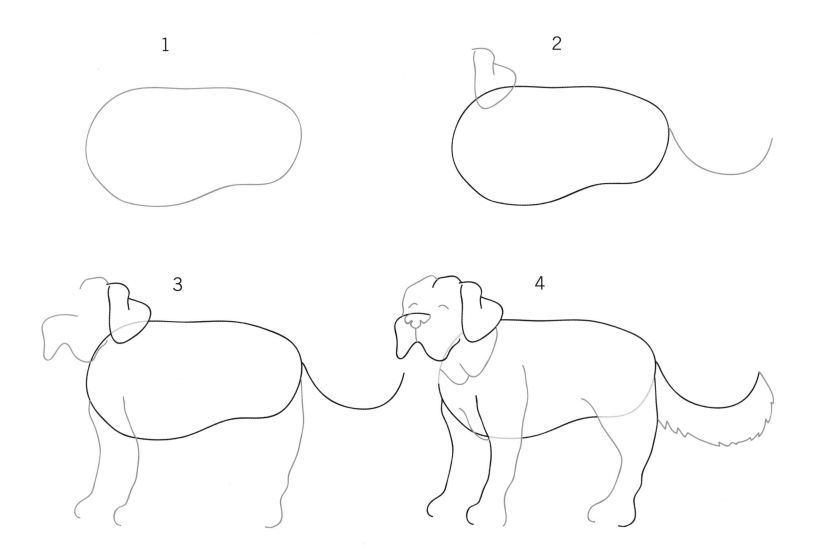

1

2

3

4

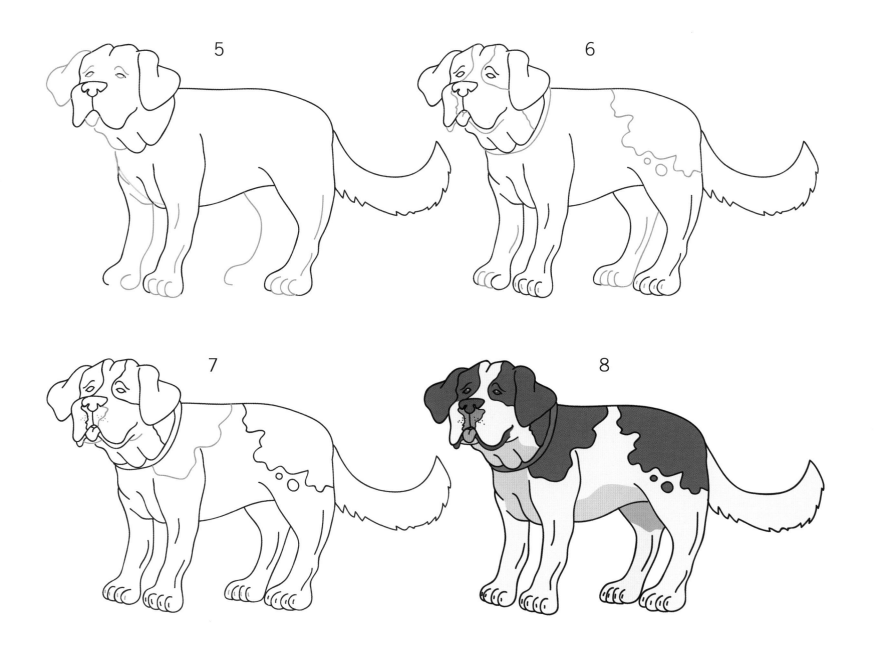

5

6

7

8

41

# Draw a Shar-Pei

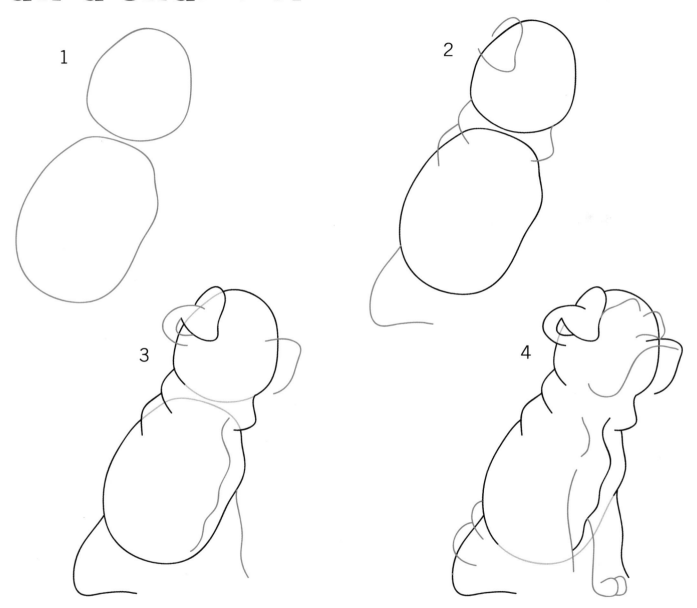

1

2

3

4

5

6

7

8

# Draw an Old English Sheepdog

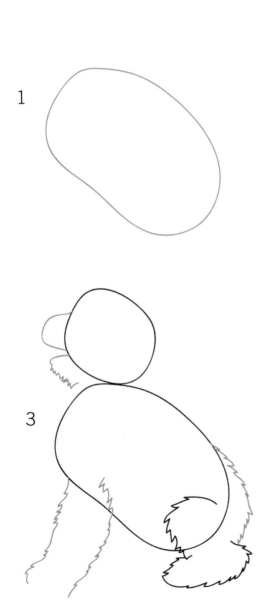

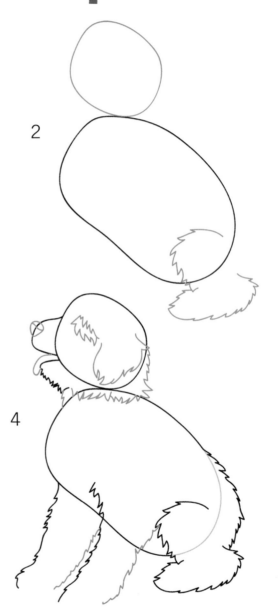

44

5

6

7

8

# Draw a Weimaraner

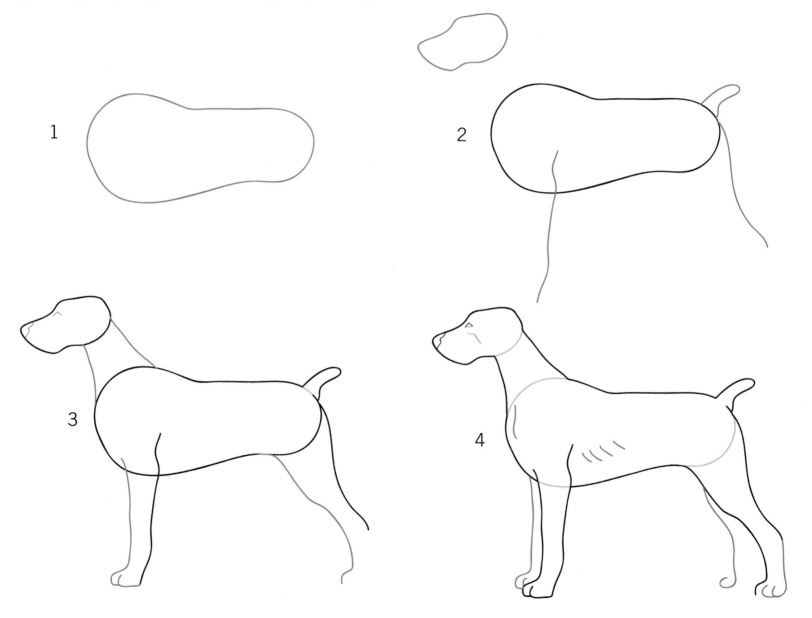

1

2

3

4

5

6

# Draw a Pug

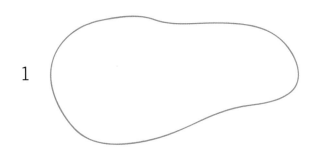

1

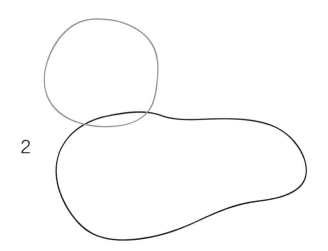

2

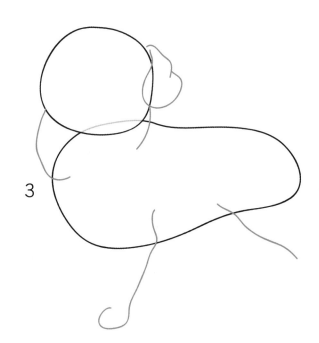

3

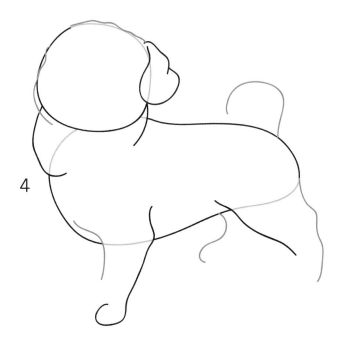

4

5

6

7

8

# Draw a Pyrenean Sheepdog

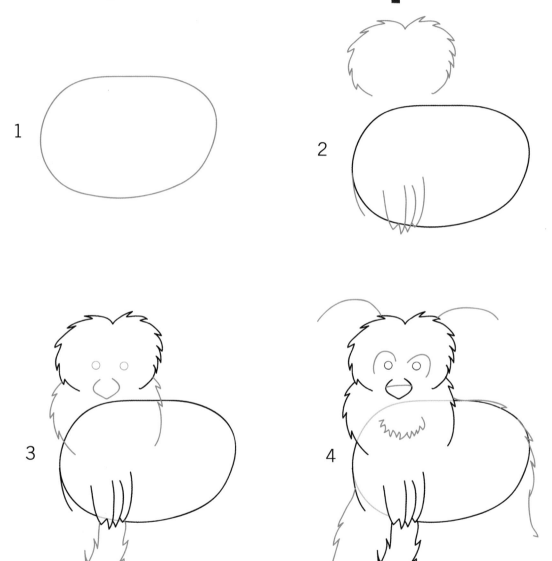

5

6

7

8

# Draw a Rottweiler

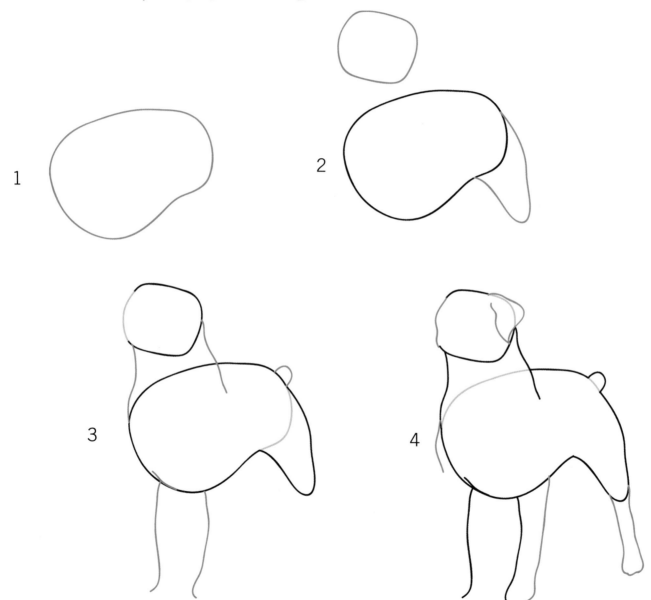

1

2

3

4

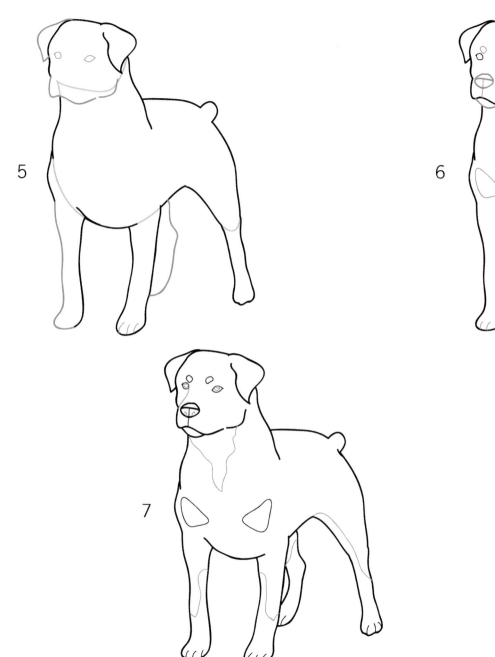

5

6

7

8

**53**

# Draw a Bulldog

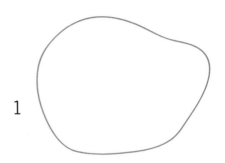

1

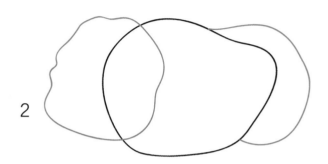

2

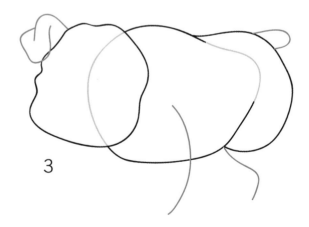

3

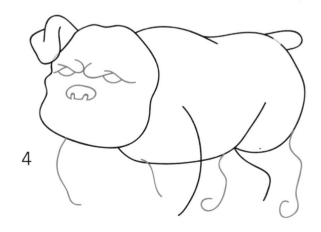

4

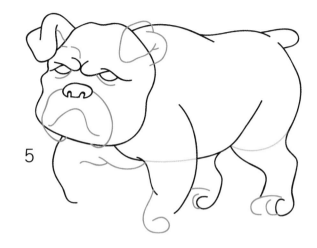

5

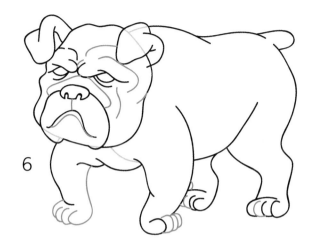

6

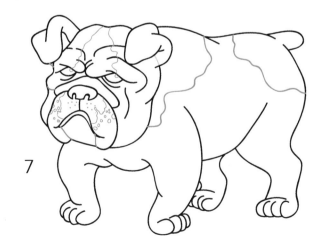

7

8

# Draw a Border Collie

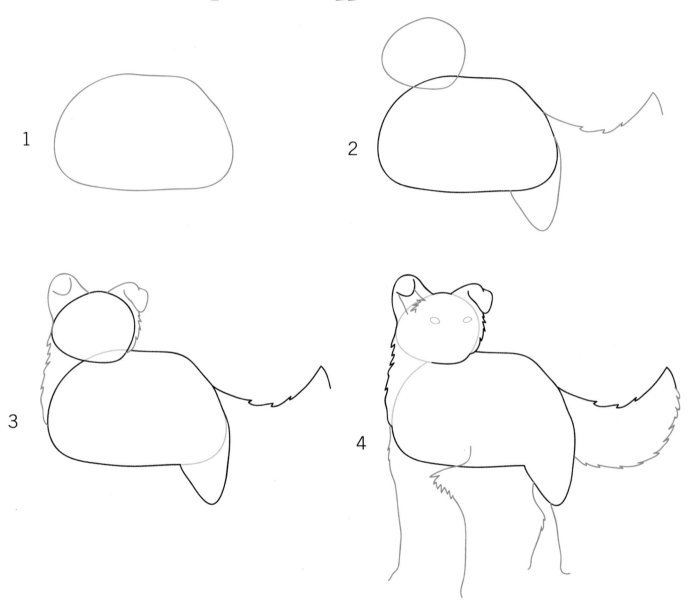

1

2

3

4

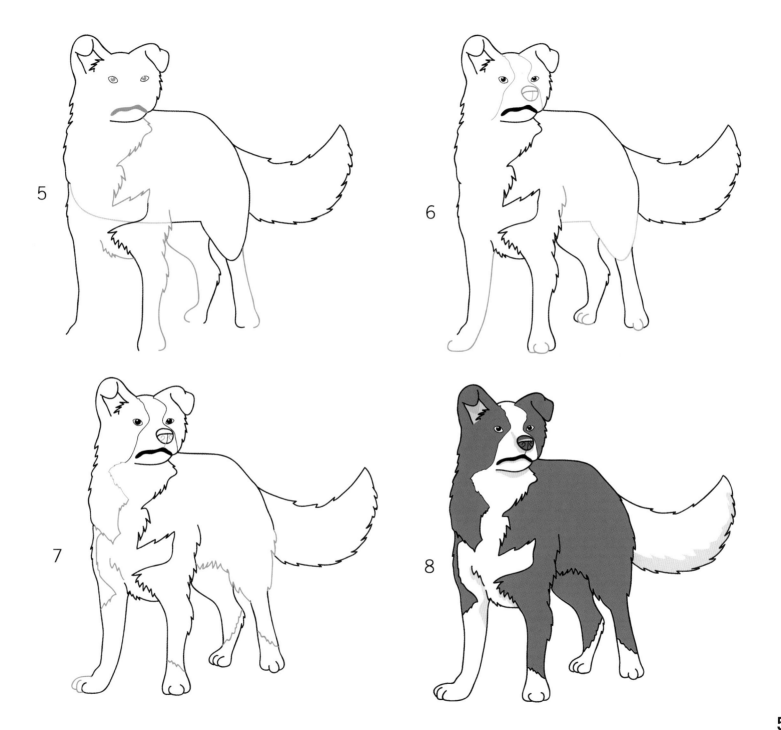

# Draw a Malinois

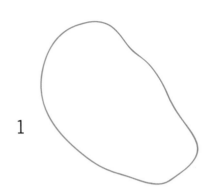

1

2

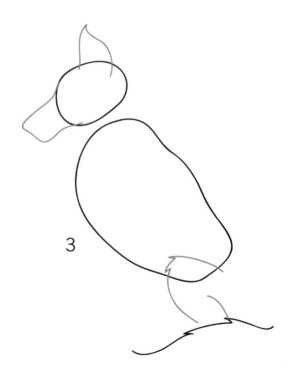

3

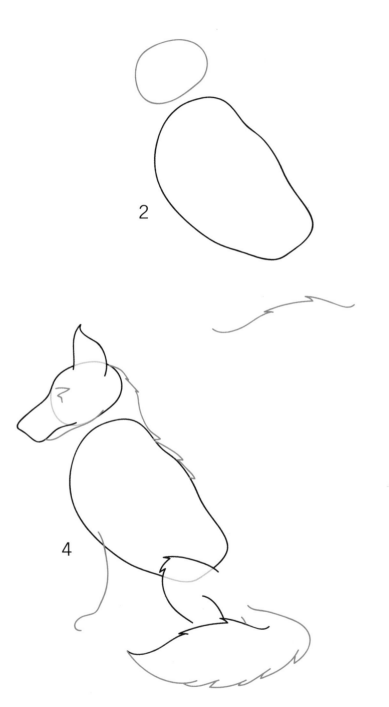

4

# Draw a Chihuahua

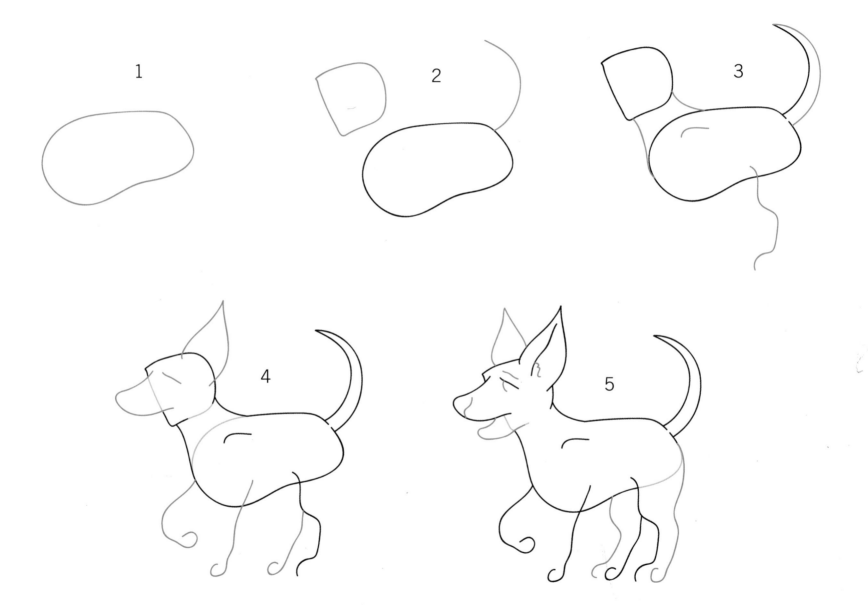

6

7

8

# Draw a Dachshund

1

2

3

4

5

6

7

# About the Artist

Steve's interest in drawing was sparked in first grade and continued all through his school years. After graduating from Capital University with a Bachelor of Fine Arts degree, Steve worked for various companies as an artist before finally deciding to head off on his own and work as a freelance illustrator. Steve has been working as a freelance illustrator for over ten years now and has over 50 children's books to his credit. He currently lives with his lovely wife, Karen, and his sheepdog, Doodle, in Columbus, Ohio.

Other Pencil, Paper, Draw!® **books to look for:**

.............................................

Pencil, Paper, Draw!® **ANIMALS**
Pencil, Paper, Draw!® **BABY ANIMALS**
Pencil, Paper, Draw!® **CARS & TRUCKS**
Pencil, Paper, Draw!® **DINOSAURS**
Pencil, Paper, Draw!® **FANTASY CREATURES**
Pencil, Paper, Draw!® **FLOWERS**
Pencil, Paper, Draw!® **HORSES**
Pencil, Paper, Draw!® **PIRATES**
Pencil, Paper, Draw!® **SHARKS**

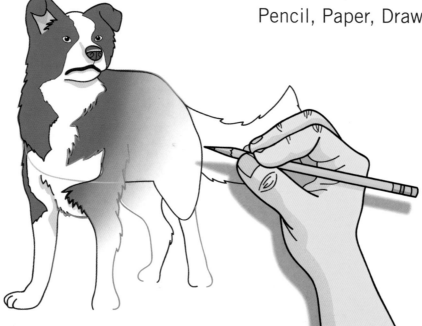